DO YOURSELF A FAVOR GET UP! AND MOVE!

Roland Ray Kangong

Do yourself a favor Get up! and Move!
Study Guide

Live your best life

You will never know you have it, until you start

Copyright © 2019 Roland Kangong
All rights reserved.

All rights reserved. This book is protected by international copyright law and may not be copied, reprinted or reproduced in any form for commercial purposes or profit. It is intended for use in youth study groups, church groups and for personal growth hence short quotations and limited copying for study purposes is permitted. All Bible quotations, unless otherwise indicated, are taken from the King James Version.

ISBN 978-0-620-85487-0

This book is for worldwide distribution

DEDICATION

To everyone with a burning desire to break free from all limitations to become who they were born to be.

Contents

How to use this book 11

Prologue: Turning your life around is possible. 12

Chapter 1 How to recognize that you indeed have a gift.
.... 17

Chapter 2 How to turn your gift into your assignment on earth 26

Chapter 3 How to work your gift to perfection. 34

Chapter 4 How to create the right environment for your gift to blossom 41

Chapter 5 How to announce yourself boldly to the world no matter what! 49

Chapter 6 How to laugh and smile through your challenges until you succeed. 55

Chapter 7 How to truly become educated 61

Chapter 8 How to recognize true success. 70

Chapter 9 How to maintain your success. 79

Chapter 10 How to remain relevant in performing your gift. 85

Preface

Knowing that you have, say a key to open a door is one thing. Knowing how to open a door with the same key is another thing. And yet, knowing what door that key can open is still something else.

Knowing that you have a gift is one thing. Knowing that your gift is indeed your life is another thing. Believing in the power of your gift is yet another thing.

This book takes you through a series of questions and reflections that will create in you a new mind and transform you into a brand-new person, ready to rock the world with your unique personality and talents. In Romans 12:1-2, it is written that you are going to experience a transformation in your life if your mind is renewed. How do you renew your mind? I believe it is possible to renew your mind through new information, new ways of thinking and acting, new associations, and

everything that prevents you from doing things the same old way you have always done.

This Study Guide is your passport to freedom, to finally break free from following the motions, from living from hand to mouth, from paycheck to paycheck, to finally be your true self.

Study it diligently, go through the questions and exercises and the rest will be history – you will indeed become a new and true you.

Roland Ray Kangong.

What's in this book?

Chapter 1 takes you through activities and information that leads you to believe that you indeed have a gift. You will be shown how to know with certainty that you are gifted.

Chapter 2 reveals the reasons you were born and how to turn your natural gifting into your assignment on earth.

Chapter 3 You will learn how to work on your gift to become the best in the world. What do you do after discovering your gift?

Chapter 4 shows you how to create the right environment for your gift to blossom. You will see what to do to stand out in the crowd.

Chapter 5 shows you how to announce yourself to the world, with or without a platform, challenges or not.

Chapter 6 will help show you how to laugh and smile through your challenges until you succeed.

Chapter 7 deals with how to become truly educated, in other words, the right education for your personal needs.

Chapter 8 looks at how to recognize true success.

Chapter 9 explores how to remain successful.

Chapter 10 explores how to remain relevant and successful after you start performing your gift.

ACKNOWLEDGMENTS

A big thank you to my siblings: Teddy, Emilly, Georges, Hosman and Willy. I love you all so dearly for your love and support. I could never ask for a better family. To my dear wife, Talence and my sons Ted-David and Jesse-Daniel, you guys are my rock. Thank you for your understanding when I am always away from home. I love you dearly.

"Finally, brethren, whatsoever things are true, whatsoever things are honest, whatsoever things are just, whatsoever things are pure, whatsoever things are lovely, whatsoever things are of good report; if there be any virtue, and if there be any praise, think on these things."

Philippians 4:8 KJV

God has given each human being 'something' to take you through life. It is called your gift and it is your responsibility to find it. Study this book, and you'll find your gift!

How to use this book

This book is intended for personal and family use, youth groups in churches and communities, schools and higher institutions.

Begin at any chapter depending on where you think you are in the journey to perfecting and using your gift.

Take time and reflect on the questions. Be sincere and honest in your answers. Think deeply and reflect on the activities. Then, you will indeed find your gift as you approach it with a new mindset that will enable you to succeed.

Prologue: Turning your life around is possible.

Core theme: Your transformation, through your gift, is guaranteed.

Principles: Your gift is always with you.

Hello everyone. Let us begin this study session by looking at our opening story, about Chris the studio owner (tell the story: he was born with an artistic gift, he did take time to develop his gift to a point of being able to use it at a professional level, since he could write catchy songs and sing pretty well. But, was he aware that he had a great gift and that he was himself a great guy?).

Activity: Think about and answer the following questions, as sincerely as possible. Be true to yourself:

How do you think Chris found out he had an artistic gift?

_____

_____

1. Why was he not using his gift profitably but rather chose odd jobs such as becoming a street sweeper? He was sitting on riches buried in his gift yet poverty was his closest associate. Why? Discuss possible reasons).
2. Now, looking at yourself, what activity/ies do you like so much that you have taken time to learn/or you are planning to start? Such an activity could be a hobby or something you want to do leisurely: write them down. Feel free to add to these suggestions.
   Sports_____

Musical/Music Instrument

_____

Design

_____

3. Take a moment to think about what you have written in (2) above. Now the question is: what motivated you to learn/want to learn that particular activity?

(**Food for thought**: Chris just didn't see his artistic gift as something that could offer him success in life; so, he looked for and worked hard at odd jobs; he wanted to make a living. But he wasted time, was getting old, and had never really had a breakthrough. Then he decided to utilize his gift – and his life was transformed). This is the case

with a lot of people, not Chris alone. **Take a moment and think about yourself or someone you know who's got a gift but is not using it. What could be possible reasons? Discuss with someone.**

4. What activity can you mention, with certainty, that you could excel at but yet like Chris, you treat it as a hobby and have neglected it?

_____

_____

Important to note: You do indeed have a gift. Do you agree with the statement? Do you disagree? Now, let's name our gifts - everyone in the room. Pick up a blank piece of paper and write down your gift/talent, something you believe you are good at or

could be good at. Make sure your neighbour doesn't see what you are writing. And please, do not discuss with your neighbour what you have written. Not yet. If you are not sure that you have a gift, write 'I don't know yet'. If there is something at the back of your mind, write "I think my gift could be…". Feel free to name more than one area of gifting. Now, let's talk!

Chapter 1 How to recognize that you indeed have a gift.

Core theme: God's purpose for your life is real (Proverbs 19:21)

Principle/s: You were born with a gift, and you have it for real. It is always tugging at you, in many ways. Pause, reflect and find it.

First, let us talk about choices. Forget about society's opinion/s of you. What are your choices? I said YOUR choices, based on your personal convictions and not someone else's opinion or suggestion. Take a moment, think about it.

There are two types of choices: those made based on a decision born out of your very personal convictions and those made based on

an external influence. For example, you may choose to study a degree in Finance and Banking because someone convinced you that it is a lucrative career path with many job offers, or you may choose to study architecture instead because you are passionate about Design, designing beautiful buildings and homes.

Where you are in life right now is a function, to a greater extent, of your decisions. Do you agree? Let's talk about today morning: you decided what time to get out of bed, what clothes and shoes to wear, what to eat for breakfast, what time to leave the house...every single action was a decision you had to make.

Now, let's look back: what or who pushed you into those decisions? Why are you studying

what you are studying or why did you study what you studied at college? Why are you wearing the outfit you have on you right now and what guided your decision to buy the outfits in your wardrobe? Did you see them on TV, on someone, or you were attracted to them at the shopping mall? Why were you attracted to the particular clothes you have bought and taken home? Was it a desire to dress to kill? Stand out in the crowd, feel good with yourself or what? To summarize, what informs your everyday choices and corresponding actions?

Your best life is tied directly to 'acting' on your gift. But, to discover your gift, to believe it is your gift and determine to use it is a CHOICE you will have to make.

Activity:

Look at and answer the following questions; be as honest as possible.

1. How do you love spending your time?
   _____
   _____

2. If you had a plan to do something or go somewhere, and your friend calls you with a different suggestion, what do you do?
   - ☐ I stick to my plan and ignore my friend.
   - ☐ I go with my friend and push my plan to some other time.
   - ☐ I convince my friend to come with me instead.

3. Do you start doing an activity and a few days/weeks/months later you feel like it

was a mistake and you decide to stop? (if yes, go to question 8)

☐ Yes

☐ No

4. If No, does that mean everything you put your mind on to accomplish, you push until is achieved?

☐ Yes

☐ No

5. If Yes, you are on the path to discovering your gift. Then go to point #11. If No, go to question 6.

6. If you answered No to question 3, do you mean that you enjoy every activity you put your mind on to do?

☐ Yes

☐ No

7. If you answered No to question 4, what makes you quit what you were so determined and excited to do? (Go to and read Chapter 6 of Do yourself a favor Get up! and Move!)

_____

_____

8. If you answered Yes to question 3, what makes you feel that way? Is it an inner voice or someone's suggestion?
   - ☐ Inner voice
   - ☐ Someone's suggestion

9. If you believe it is your inner voice, does this happen to you all the time in almost everything you do?
   - ☐ Yes (if yes, go to and read Chapter 3, otherwise continue)
   - ☐ No

10. If your answer to question 8 is 'someone's suggestion', patiently go through the entire book Do yourself a favor Get up! and Move! because you do not believe in yourself, in your Creator and the gift He has freely given to you.

11. Last and most importantly, if you believe you were born with a gift, write down your thoughts. Think of and start working on an action plan. To assist you, go through Chapter 1 of the book again).

_____

_____

_____

_____

Think about this:

If the decisions you make in life are influenced by someone or some event or the media, chances are that you have not listened to your inner voice: the voice of your spirit that is forever pointing you to your calling in life.

If what you are identifying as your gift comes from within you, from that inner voice, and you are determined to carry it out irrespective of what anybody else thinks about it, even if you are laughed at, then you have found your gift or you might be very close to finding it.

Take a pen and notebook, or use your hand-held device and write it down boldly; and start to think about it and see yourself

far into the future, where you want to be with that gift because, as we are going to see next, that gift is your assignment on planet earth; it is the reason you were born.

Chapter 2 How to turn your gift into your assignment on earth.

*Core theme: Your **gift** is your **life**!*

*Principle: Believe in your gift (talent, calling, potential), pursue it relentlessly, make the right choices and **avoid procrastination, laziness and comfort**.*

In this chapter, I want to state categorically that you indeed have a gift that you were born with. It is not a matter of debate and it is not to be doubted. If you think you are not gifted, it is probably because you are failing to 'see' the gift that is always with you, every single day of your life, probably because it is something you can do with a lot of ease.

Let us start by looking critically at the story of a young boy called Dada and his dad Mike and

mom Rhoda (tell the story). Mike and Rhoda were school drop outs. Dropping out of school is a recipe for failure, for most people especially in Third World countries, because there is a stereotyped belief on what it takes to succeed in life: *go to school, get a qualification and get a job.*

Life is not and cannot be lived in a single day. There is a popular saying that Rome was not built in a day, but truly, those who spend so much time building do so because they believe in what they are doing. If Mike and Rhoda could become so successful, using their God-given abilities, what is stopping anyone from succeeding in life?

Ponder on these: *believe in and make a choice to pursue your gifting; realize you are not the only one with that gift but that yours is unique because you are unique, so never*

compare yourself with some like-gifted individual; do not procrastinate; hate comfort with a passion if you want to succeed; develop a deep love for your gift (Darn discovered himself in the act (page 52)).

Activity:

Look at and answer the following questions. Be honest with yourself.

1. By now, do you believe you have a gift?
   ☐ Yes
   ☐ No
2. If Yes, can you talk about it openly to anyone with no reservations?
   ☐ Yes
   ☐ No
3. If you answered 'No' to 1, write down any/all activities that interest you in life.
   _____
   _____
   _____

4. Look carefully at your response to 3. Can you see one activity that immensely interests you or that 'pops out' of the page? Think again and write down your thoughts. Save/keep in a safe place what you have written for future reference.

5. If you answered 'No' to 2, why can't you speak openly about that which you consider your gift?

_____

_____

_____

6. Again, in 5, do you feel embarrassed to tell someone about the activity you most cherish? I know, because most people would rather talk about school

---

qualifications than gifts. What is going on in your mind?

_____

_____

_____

_____

7. Looking back into the chapter, if you were Mike or Rhoda, would you be ashamed that you never completed school and become discouraged to the point that you see yourself as useless in life?

   ☐ Yes

   ☐ No

8. If you answered Yes to 7, then what you are embarrassed of might very likely be your gift because even though your society makes you feel uncomfortable

about it, you still want to pursue it. What you need is the right environment (read Chapter 4) as you perfect your gift (read Chapter 3).

If you answered No to 7, then you are on the right path. Start perfecting your gift (read Chapter 3 again).

9. Do you sometimes look at yourself and compare yourself to others and wish you were someone else? Or, do you sometimes see everyone else in a better position in life than you are?

☐ Yes

☐ No

Explain your answer, why Yes or No.

_____

_____

10. Do you admire successful sports, film, music, TV etc stars?

    ☐ Yes

    ☐ No

    Explain your answer. Why?

11. Your favourite actor, sportsman/woman, TV star etc. could have succeeded in another career e.g Venus Williams could have been a successful accountant. Why do you think she stuck to the gift that has made her a wealthy star today?

_____
_____
_____
_____

12. Do you feel a deep desire on the inside to stick to your gift?

  ☐ Yes
  ☐ No

  If Yes, you are on the right path. If No, re-think what you want to do with your life and write it down (for future reference).

13. Most importantly, think deeply and see if you could be willing to drop everything else and follow this dream in your heart if you didn't have bills to pay for a time. Write down your thoughts.

Your gift should be so important to you that if you had your way, you would drop every other activity and pursue it with everything you got. Pursuing your gift with a competing activity that takes most of your time may slow you down, but you won't mind working on your gift late into the night. Think about it.

Chapter 3 How to work your gift to perfection.

Core theme: Your gift requires hard, smart work in order for you to be able to perform it at the most excellent level!

Principle: Work, work and work some more but, work right!

Question: Do you believe you stand a chance among 7 billion inhabitants on earth to be noticed? Take a moment and think about this.

Question: Is it about getting noticed or is it about just succeeding in your own little corner and making enough to get by, day by day?

Possible answers: Absolutely yes. You stand a chance in a billion people. If there was

---

someone existing with your same finger prints, I'd dare say you do not stand a chance.

It is not about getting noticed or getting by. It is about realizing that you were born to make a difference, even as you stand out in the crowd, in your 'little' corner.

Question: How is that possible?

Possible answer: Through perfection, working on a gift with the aim of becoming the best at it!

Activity

Fill in the spaces. Provide honest answers.

1. Since you are convinced you have found your gift, how many hours out of the 24hours/day are devoted SOLELY to

working on it?

_____

2. When you feel down and out, depressed, discouraged by life, does the thought of your gift raise hope in you?
    - ☐ Yes
    - ☐ Sometimes
    - ☐ Maybe
    - ☐ No

3. Think carefully about your answer to 2 above and briefly explain your choice:

_____
_____
_____
_____

- Here are my thoughts on the possible answers to 2

- Yes – suggests that you truly believe you have found an activity you could bet your life on. Such a stance places you automatically on the path to success provided you embrace the whole package as explained in the chapters in this book.
- Sometimes – is an indication that you have this gift at the back of your mind but there are other competing priorities that tend to take away your attention. It could be your job, family, a need in your life, stuff you are dealing with and so on. Remember: your attitude towards stuff in your life has a 90% impact on how you'll be able to come out of it.
- Maybe – clearly says you are not even convinced about this gift story. You are

---

probably a Doubting Thomas and believe in what you can see and touch. Until your mindset changes, you will continue to go through the motions and erroneously believe that your job is your gift or calling in life.

- No – highly suggests that you have not yet found your gift, or you probably do not believe in gifts; you are likely the go-to-school-and-get-a-good-job kind of person. Or, you are one of those people who have chosen to just exist, and pass through life, bemoaning your fate and forever wishing something good will come your way.

Whatever the category of answer you may find yourself in, the whole truth is

that you have a gift and you need to search for it with everything you have, because your life depends on it (Go back and read Chapters 1 & 2).

4. Do you know that working on your gift means a whole lot of things?
   Write down what you understand by *working* on a gift (your answer should have at least 8 – 10 points).

   _____
   _____
   _____
   _____

5. Go through the points you have listed in 4. Look carefully at them, one by one, and honestly see if you have been diligent at improving yourself along the

lines of your gift or not. Causal, every now and then kind of approach to work will take you nowhere with your gift. Do you agree? Discuss with a partner.

6. How deliberate and diligent are you at working to perfect your gift? Are you determined to succeed no matter what may come your way? If your answer is Yes, read Chapter 6 again. If your answer is No, read through the entire book slowly, chapter by chapter, then come back to this page in the Study Guide and continue to the next chapter.

Perfection is the one thing that allows you to make a quantum leap from mediocrity to stardom (Michael Jackson)

Chapter 4 How to create the right environment for your gift to blossom

Core theme: Surround yourself with the right people, go to the right places, think the right thoughts, read the right books and watch inspiring movies, tv programs and visuals that bring value to your dreams; moreover, speak the right words, if you want to succeed!

Principle: Watch your company (friends, acquaintances and media sources)!

A popular saying goes: Bad company corrupts good manners.

In this book we say: Bad company destroys beautiful gifts.

In high school, we had a teacher who always said: be at the right place, at the

right time, doing the right thing! Don't you agree?

Activity

Consider the following questions about your close friends and your habits. Be honest!

1. Who is your best friend and why?
   _____
   _____

2. How well do you know your best friend? Think slowly and hard.

3. Have you and your best friend ever had disagreements? If yes, how do you resolve your differences?
   _____
   _____
   _____

_____

4. Have you ever taken time to evaluate your friendship to find out if it is not due to some activity you enjoy together, such as drinking or shopping, or do you inspire each other to do positive things in life? Think carefully about this and discuss.

5. Is your friendship symbiotic or parasitic? Now, you need to be truly honest with your answer here. (Think of friends who only hang around you when the going is good and those who stick by you even in bad times).

   _____
   _____
   _____

6. When you encounter problems in your life, how do your friends respond? Do

they show concern, stick around you, spend time with you and encourage you, or do they call you on the phone, ask how you are doing and start talking about their own problems? Think hard and be honest.

_____
_____
_____
_____

7. How much time do you spend on your smartphone? And doing what exactly? Be honest. Get a piece of paper and write down times spent holding or looking at the screen of your phone, just the same way you record car mileage. For example, before you go on Facebook in the morning, check the time. If it is

05h00 for example, write down 05h00. If you log out of Facebook at 05h30, write down the time. Record that as entry #1. Do that for all your smartphone usage. See the example below:

Date: 01/12/2018

05h00 – 05h40 Facebook

06h00 – 06h10 WhatsApp

06h15 – 06h23 Auntie's phone call

08h11 – 09h00 Twitter etc.

At the end of the week, add the total number of minutes spent on your phone, divide by 60 to find out how many hours you spend on the phone. Then, ask yourself this important question in 8:

8. Of the entire time spent on my smartphone, how much of that time had to do with my gift?

   _____

   _____

   _____

9. Seriously, is the environment surrounding you, by yourself, at work, school or elsewhere, favorable to the growth of your gift? Be honest with yourself.

10. How many hours a day are devoted to working on your gift, in such a way that you do not tolerate any distractions e.g you switch off or keep away your smartphone?

    _____

    _____

11. Are you satisfied with your answer to 10 above? If Yes, can you show proof of improvement in your gift? If No, read Chapter 4 all over again and decide to devote meaningful time to developing your gift/talent (see Chapter 3).

12. After considering all of the above questions, can you truthfully say you have created a conducive environment around yourself for success at what you want to achieve? Write down your thoughts honestly.

_____

_____

_____

13. People have a tendency to always talk about their passions and interests. For example, soccer lovers talk soccer;

Formula 1 lovers talk cars and racing; bookworms talk academics; sport lovers talk about their preferred sport and each of these groups watch related TV shows, read relevant books and magazines. What do you read, watch or talk about that directly relates to your gift?

_____

_____

_____

14. Are your best friends passionate about the same things in life as you are, or are they a distraction to you and your gift? Be honest and think about this deeply.

Surround yourself, fill your mind, spend your time, read about, watch and talk about your gift and you will be influential in life.

Chapter 5 How to announce yourself boldly to the world no matter what!

Core theme: You have a gift and the world needs to see and hear you. This is no time for timidity, fear or worrying about what people are going to say or think. It's YOUR time, to get up and start moving. Start showing the world what you have, who you truly are!

Principle: Get up and start moving! Start sharing your gift with the world.

A gifted singer who has not released an album or is not singing at gigs or at church and social gatherings simply is not existing. A gifted footballer who is not training and showing his skills to potential clubs is as good as not existing. A gifted designer who is not designing and showing off his/her products is

as good as not existing. Do you see what I mean? If you are not showing off your gift, if you are not performing your gift, it is as if you do not exist (because no one knows you!), that's what I mean.

Activity

Consider the following questions and be honest with yourself as you answer because ***self-deception is a destroyer of gifts and lives #RolandRayK***.

1. Are you and introvert or an extrovert?
2. Think carefully about your response to 1 above. Have you ever had an embarrassing moment? Mention it and say why you think it was embarrassing.

_____

_____

3. Looking at 2 above, don't you think your embarrassing moment could be because you are a shy person? Or maybe because you are a proud person?

   _____

   _____

4. Do you bother about what people think of you? Maybe you are always preoccupied with what people will say about your dressing, hairstyle, colour of your suit or dress etc?

   _____

   _____

5. Are you able to stand up in front of a crowd of people and talk to them even if they boo at you?
   - ☐ Yes
   - ☐ No

6. Do you find your heart beating faster or do you find yourself sweating if you are asked to maybe come to the front of a class, church, or conference room for example, and speak?
    - ☐ Yes
    - ☐ No
7. If you answered Yes to 5, and No to 6 above, then you are bold and fearless and, on your way to expressing your gift openly. If you answered No to 5 above, and Yes to 6 above, read Chapter 5 of the book again, slowly and deliberately.
8. What type of person are you when it comes to giving?
    - ☐ Open-handed
    - ☐ Tight-fisted (selfish)

9. Do you find it easier to give to someone related to you only or would you give to or help a complete stranger? Think about this.

10. Would you give your last dollar to a mother with a baby on the street crying of hunger? Think before you answer.

11. Performing your gift is a way to share what you received from God with the world. Do you realize that? Think about it.

12. At this point, make a plan, a kind of calendar of events, to start showcasing your gift. For instance, make up your mind to join the choir, start a singing group, perform for free at birthdays/parties, start running every

week, buy even cheap material if you have little money and start designing your clothes, shoes, handbags etc. I mean, find a way to start. Use a format like this one suggested:

Event	Date
Loic's birthday Friday 20th	Perform 2 songs acapella
Saturday mornings 0500 - 0700	Run from home to CBD and back
Daily 1900 - 2100	Work on my designs

You see what I mean? Create a plan like the table above and be able to track your progress. That is a sure way to start telling the world that you exist.

Most importantly, BE CONSISTENT!

Chapter 6 How to laugh and smile through your challenges until you succeed.

Core theme: Your thoughts affect your actions and your actions directly determine the outcomes in your life. Do you agree?

Principle: Do you want to win in life? Then, learn to develop a thick skin!

A wise man once said that when you have a problem, the manner in which you look at that problem, especially in your mind, determines how quick a solution may be found. Ain't that so true?

Activity

Let us consider the following questions and scenarios.

1. Do you smile or laugh very often? What makes you smile or laugh?

   _____
   _____
   _____
   _____

2. Do you smile at people when you talk to or greet them whether it is someone you know or a complete stranger?

   _____
   _____
   _____

3. Do you enjoy jokes, even so-called expensive jokes?

   _____
   _____
   _____

4. Do you easily get upset especially when something is said or done around you that you do not like, or do you just smile and ignore it? Think about it carefully and write down your answer, explaining why you get upset or not.

_____

5. So, having thought about and answered the above four questions, can you now say to which of 3 groups you belong?
    - ☐ I enjoy laughter and smiling, even if someone tries to annoy me.
    - ☐ I easily get upset and angry even at little things that I could have ignored.
    - ☐ Whether I laugh and smile or not depends on my mood and the

circumstances surrounding me at a given moment.

6. How do you handle criticism? Please be honest with yourself.

   _____

   _____

7. Now, have you found your gift yet?
   - ☐ Yes
   - ☐ No

8. If you answered yes to 7 above, are you very passionate and excited about your gift to the point of talking about it and wanting to show/tell people around you about it?
   - ☐ Yes
   - ☐ No

9. If you answered Yes to 8, what do you do if you excitedly start talking about your gift and someone tells you that you are stupid, or you have missed your way in life, or you are a frustrated jerk? Do you get angry, discouraged, concur with them, or you just look at them and smile and walk away, or do you try to explain to them what your gift is all about? Think hard about this scenario. If you answered No to 8, do you mean that you feel shy or ashamed to talk about your gift, or you avoid talking about it because you feel embarrassed, or you are avoiding getting angry especially if someone comments negatively about your gift? Think on this carefully.

Discuss these points with some like-minded peer.

10.   Are you that type of person that you don't care what anyone says or thinks about you and your gift, but you keep on doing what you are convinced you ought to be doing with a smile on your face? Look inward at yourself.

It is very important to laugh. It is very important to smile. This must happen irrespective of the circumstances around you. Science tells us that smiling, and laughter have tremendous health benefits while anger and frowning destroy health. You need your health to succeed at your gifting in life.

Laugh and smile through all challenges that come your way. That's a sure recipe for victory

Chapter 7 How to truly become educated

Core theme: Find your gift, but not only that, educate yourself on your gift if you hope to perform it at the best possible level and stand out of the crowd.

> *Principle: Study to show yourself approved... (2 Timothy 2: 15) in everything, even your gift.*

Question: Which is more important, skills or certificates?

Think about it. Consider the activities and scenarios below. Make sure you listen to your inner voice and follow your gut feeling. Remember, "...keep your heart with all diligence; for out of it are the issues of life" (Proverbs 4:23). Also remember Proverbs 3:

5-6, "*5 Trust in the Lord with all thine heart; and lean not unto thine own understanding. 6 In all thy ways acknowledge him, and he shall direct thy paths*".

As you listen to your inner voice, trust the Lord to guide your decisions and actions.

Activity:

1. In your opinion, what do you understand by the term education? Discuss with your friends or in your youth group.

2. The term "education" is generally associated with attending a school, passing exams and getting a certificate. What do you think? Write down your thoughts after careful thinking and discussions with your friend/s.

   _____
   _____

_____

3. Would you say learning to ride a bicycle or driving a car or playing the piano is equivalent to getting an education? Think about it and write down your thoughts.

   _____

4. Talking about schooling, at what level of studying are you right now?
   - ☐ Still in school (primary, high school, tertiary).
   - ☐ Dropped out of school due to lack of financial support but wish I could go back.
   - ☐ Dropped out of school to pursue my dream career.
   - ☐ Never been to school, really since there was no one to help me.
   - ☐ Completed school and looking for a job.
   - ☐ Completed, found a job but I hate this job.

- ☐ Completed school but not sure what I can or want to do.
- ☐ Completed school but wish I could study further.
- ☐ Completed school but my certificate/diploma/degree feels like a mistake.
- ☐ Studying by myself towards some qualification.
- ☐ Doing an online course.
- ☐ Not really sure what I want in life hence am doing nothing, hoping something comes up.

5. Looking at 4 above, there is need to consider all the points with the help of a youth leader, youth Pastor, parent or teacher, mentor or an adult if you are a teenager. Take a closer look at the box

you ticked above. No matter what box you ticked, the principal question is: have you figured out what your gift is since you started reading the book Do yourself a favor Get up! and Move! up to this chapter?

☐ Yes

☐ No

6. If you answered Yes to 5, go ahead to 7. If you answered No to 5, make a note in your study guide, and go back to the book, and begin reading patiently again from Chapter 1.

7. How do you split your time daily between the other things you are doing and working on your gift? In other

words, are your hours structured daily, like 0800 – 1430 (School), 1500 – 1700 (school assignments/ house chores) 1800 – 1900 (working out at the basketball court) etc? as already indicated in Chapters 4 & 5 of this study guide? You see, you can't do things randomly, going with the flow and doing whatever you choose at any given time. So, do you have a consistent or almost consistent pattern of doing things daily? A wise man once said that *you will excel at what you do consistently, not what you do from time to time*.

8. Concerning your gift, how are you improving your knowledge and skills?

- ☐ I watch YouTube videos.
- ☐ I have a mentor.

- ☐ I have friends that we practice/study/discuss/work together.
- ☐ I read books related to my gift, e.g.(name the book/s)

_____

_____

_____

- ☐ I read magazines related to my gift, e.g. (name them)

_____

- ☐ I think about my gift and what the future holds for me.

9. Do you ever write down your thoughts? Or, when you watch a video, listen to a podcast or attend a conference/talk show etc, do you write down points you find relevant to your gift? Doing so or not has serious implications. Think about it.

10. You hear some people say that they don't have to write notes because they always remember what they are listening to or watching, yet science tells us that after 6 days the average human being forgets 75% of what they heard. You need to discuss with your group and from this day, start keeping a notebook where you write down ideas daily, better still get a diary. After 4 weeks, meet again as a group and look back at everything you wrote.

Keep revisiting your ideas and that will keep you focused. Without *focus*, you would be like a ship sailing by following

whatever direction the wind blows, with no destination in mind.

After you have discovered your gift and started to develop it and you are educating yourself along those lines, remember you are developing yourself, to be yourself, and not a copy of someone else. Aspire to play basketball like Kevin Durant, do not try to become Kevin Durant, because you can NEVER be someone else.

Chapter 8 How to recognize true success.

Core theme: Success has different definitions for different people. Whatever your definition of success, do not forget that every human being has 24 hours a day. Successful people are those who find their gift, consciously and deliberately use the 24 hours of each day to develop it until that point where they start to bless the world with it.

Principle: Find your gift, develop it, and start blessing the world with it. Keep developing your gift, strive for excellence and never feel you have 'arrived'. In other words, refuse to stop learning and growing; then, that would mark the beginning of your own success story.

1. If you are asked what you would like to achieve in your lifetime to consider yourself successful, what would that be?

_____

_____

_____

2. What have you done in your life that you see as success? It could be something as simple as learning to ride a bicycle or even falling in love with someone you have always admired.

3. What type of people would you consider successful?
   ☐ Rich people such as politicians, businessmen etc.
   ☐ Celebrities.
   ☐ Anyone with a permanent job.
   ☐ Anyone working.

☐ Anyone living in their own house and not renting.

☐ Someone owning an expensive car.

Justify your answer in a few words

_____

_____

_____

4. I believe that by now you have figured out what your gift could be. I mean, that activity you are willing to embark on for the rest of your life.

How passionate are you about it?

☐ Very passionate

☐ I think about it all the time

☐ I speak about it all the time

☐ I research about it all the time

☐ I watch videos about it all the time

- ☐ I wake up in the morning thinking about it
- ☐ I go to sleep at night feeling good about it

Note that your success begins when you embrace your gift with conviction and are ready to make it your life's dream and reason for living.

5. When moments of doubt and discouragement arise, either from some inner voice or someone on the outside who feels you are wasting your time talking about succeeding in a gift, how do you handle such?

_____
_____
_____
_____

6. Do you value the little steps you take each day towards success with your dream or do you feel sometimes like you're groping in the dark and want to give up? Honestly write down the conflicts in your mind that you deal with daily as you pursue your gifting.

_____
_____

7. Do you firmly believe that you have the tenacity to carry on despite things looking contrary to your expectations? In other words, have you made up your mind to pursue your dream no matter the challenges until you succeed?

_____
_____
_____

8. This is all about becoming excellent at what you do. That's a good way to become valuable. In your mind, do you see yourself becoming so good that people who need someone with your gift/skills/talents will come looking for you? Think deep and hard and be able to see in your imagination where you want to go and who you want to become! Discuss in your group.

(Steve Harvey once said, in response to Hebrews 11:1b ("...faith is the evidence of things not seen...") that the evidence is in your imagination. Think about it. Every great invention and human innovation and technological discoveries started in someone's mind, as an imagined thought. Think deeply about this.)

9. Talking about careers in life, do you see any distinction between a gift and a career determined by college qualifications?

10. Whether you answered yes or no, if you have indeed identified your gift, are you able to see in what ways your college qualification could add value to your gift? (Someone may say I qualified as an accountant and now I want to be producing movies. Where is the connection?) Look carefully, the connection is there. What did you find?

_____
_____
_____
_____

_____

11. We all need money for all the right or wrong reasons. Do you focus on looking for and getting involved in an activity that's going to make you money for your bills rather than focus on some gift with no clear idea how its going to make money for you? Explain your position in a few words.

_____
_____
_____
_____

When ideas of some activity or invention pop into your mind, do you take time to think about it or do you immediately google the idea and follow someone's thoughts on the internet about it, or do you shut every other voice and listen to your inner voice talking to you about

it? This is a very important point. Some have clearly 'seen' their gift in their mind's eyes, but because it is not something familiar or something they can read about on the internet, they discard it. Think on these things!

12. Has any new idea ever popped into your mind and you ignored it because it wasn't familiar?

_____
_____
_____

Success is doing what you love if and only if it is benefitting the world and lifting up other human beings to become better. If you love, for example, lies and stealing and even if you are good at it, that is NOT success.

Chapter 9 How to maintain your success.

Core theme: Have you heard of a phrase called 'staying power'? Have you seen, or do you know someone who is broke today but used to be rich, in fact, very rich some years back? Can you recall big names in sports and music for example, that were the talk of the day but just disappeared and you never heard of them again? Think on these questions.

Principle: Find your gift, develop it, love it, live it and STAY successful.

Question: Is it possible to stay successful? Emphatically yes. Is it easy? Yes and no. It depends.

1. Have you ever looked and someone rich, especially someone your age or younger than you and felt bad? Yes/No? Justify your answer.

   _____
   _____
   _____

2. Do you believe life is unfair? Explain.

   _____
   _____

3. Have you ever taken some action or said something, and people clapped hands for you and told you how great a person you are? If yes, how did you feel after such comments?

   _____
   _____

4. How did you feel if you give a good performance at your gift and no one seems to bother? Think about it.
5. Did you feel empty and wonder why they are clapping for you or did you feel like a true star?

_____

6. Did it occur to you that the reason they clapped for you could be linked to your gift? Think carefully.
7. Did you feel very grateful to God and felt proud of yourself and forever felt like you were the best at that action for which you received a standing ovation? Think on your answer.

_____
_____
_____

8. If you felt great after being told that you are good at something, did you get back to work and really worked hard to become better at it or did you find no need for hard work since you were already recognized by the particular group of persons as the best?

_____
_____
_____

9. If you are in sports, for example, how many times have you challenged yourself by going the extra mile during practice, adding an extra 5kg to your weights in the gym during workouts, or increasing your running distance?

_____

You see, your body quickly adjusts to new challenges thrown at it; and if you do not constantly do something different, you will think you are still good at what you do, which may not necessarily be true.

10. So, do you now realize your level of performing your gift may diminish if you don't keep working?

_____
_____
_____

11. How enthusiastic are you about your gift? Is the desire for it still burning in your heart like it used to before? Are you still as excited as much about your gift? Please, answer honestly.

_____
_____

12. If you answered 'no' to 11, or even hesitated to answer, chances are that you are losing interest in your gift. That is a sure way for your performance of that skill to drop, with the implication that you may not stay successful. In the book we read about Michael Jordan, who although was already a celebrated basketball star, he still practiced 10 hours everyday. No wonder he stayed successful for his entire career. Think on these things.

Immerse yourself in your gift, stay connected with the right people, listen to the right stuff on radio, tv, podcasts etc, watch the right TV programs, watch the right movies, read relevant information, keep on practicing as if you are just starting. If you do that, you are guaranteed to remain relevant, and you will stay successful.

Chapter 10 How to remain relevant in performing your gift.

Core theme: Keeping yourself relevant, loving what you do and doing what you love, connecting with people, holding someone else's hand and lifting them up, living for humanity rather than selfishly, in love and truth, is who you are after all.

Principle: Reach out to the world with your gift, hold someone's hand, lead, love and help them. That's what you were born to do.

1. Think of the journey you have walked so far. I am not saying you have arrived, not yet, but having found and convinced

yourself as to what your gift really is, is the beginning of arriving at that place where you can start living your best life. Is that where you are right now? Write down your honest thoughts.

_____
_____
_____

2. Are you multi-gifted? List all your gifts.

_____
_____

3. If you really had to make a choice, and there's nothing you could do to alter such a request, which of your gifts would be your number 1? Why?

_____
_____

4. If you have a job, are in school or at home wondering when you will start making money from your new-found gift, how does that make you feel?

_____

_____

_____

5. At this stage, the idea of your gift, talking about it and studying, working and thinking about it has probably taken over your entire being. Is that the case with you? Explain how you feel about your gift.

Let your gift consume you. Have a burning passion for it. Live it, sleep it, eat it, drink it, speak it, BE it! Permanently.

www.ingramcontent.com/pod-product-compliance
Lightning Source LLC
Chambersburg PA
CBHW031456040426
42444CB00007B/1123